A Quiet Time with Quotes

Nancy Winningham

A Quiet Time with Quotes

Nancy Winningham

authorHOUSE®

AuthorHouse™ LLC
1663 Liberty Drive
Bloomington, IN 47403
www.authorhouse.com
Phone: 1-800-839-8640

Published by AuthorHouse 01/22/2014

ISBN: 978-1-4918-5418-1 (sc)
ISBN: 978-1-4918-5419-8 (e)

Library of Congress Control Number: 2014901009

Acknowledgements

There are many people who have dedicated time, encouragement, and love during the advancement of this magnificent accomplishment and they are worthy of the acknowledgement. First, I will acknowledge God, who has given me the words, wisdom, strength, and knowledge to begin and complete this book, without God it would have been impossible for me to organize a book such as this. A book of quotes which will allow all who reads each one of them to have a quiet time with them all. Due to the different test of greatness that has come upon me during my journey I was still able to provide an eminence of moving quotes because of these individuals. Their assurance in me forms the inspiration within my soul to convey these moving words to you. I will forever be grateful for all the suggestions that were given to me while being able to accept corrective criticism. Thank you to all of my wonderful family and friends for your support.

Dedication

There are some extraordinary people I would like to dedicate this book to:

To the marvelous love of my life Fredrick Wayne Hurt Winningham, who continues to be my motivator, considerate, truthful, honorable, upstanding, and devoted since the day we met. I love you my Sweetie Pie, thank you for loving me, and thank you for being the inspiration that I always need.

To my oldest son Gregory Sherman Lawrence, whom has always inspired me to make every effort to accomplish my goals. Thank you for showing yourself to be a responsible and productive young man. I love you and may God continue to surround you with the spirit of protection.

To my youngest son Thomias Jeremy Hughes, who has always stated such reassuring words to me. Thank you for being so loving, honest, and giving me such big hugs on a daily basis. I love you my little man, my future attorney, and basketball player.

You don't know my story, you only see
how God has enlarged my territory!

~Nancy Winningham~

God keeps blessing in the right direction.
~Nancy Winningham~

It is praying time and not playing time.
~Nancy Winningham~

I have to go through a process
before I can gain progress.

~Nancy Winningham~

The Holy Spirit will lead me
where man can never go.

~Nancy Winningham~

Make no room for distraction when you are expecting a positive reaction.

~Nancy Winningham~

When God brings you to it just praise your way through it.

~Nancy Winningham~

Let your journey be the roadmap
toward accomplishments.

~Nancy Winningham~

Stop stressing while waiting
on your blessing.

~Nancy Winningham~

Always expect the expected.
~Nancy Winningham~

No matter how big or small God
is the originator of it all!
~Nancy Winningham~

I have an option to make my
faith or break my faith.

~Nancy Winningham~

When I acknowledge that I am
fed up God will fix it up.

~Nancy Winningham~

Stop stressing while the enemy
is messing, just remember in the
middle of it all God is blessing.

~Nancy Winningham~

Pray before you say because in the
midst of it all God is making a way.

~Nancy Winningham~

Faith shows assurance while
anticipation brings doubt.

~Nancy Winningham~

I am not faultless but I
am blessed by God.

~Nancy Winningham~

When God provides the direction and
you don't follow the right path,
it is no one's fault but your
own when you get lost.
~Nancy Winningham~

I am not just a receiver, I am a believer.
~Nancy Winningham~

Change is an open door for
you to walk through.

~Nancy Winningham~

Procrastination makes you lose
focus on your destination.

~Nancy Winningham~

Willing worker, willing heart.
~Nancy Winningham~

I am thankful to God for
correlating my life.
~Nancy Winningham~

Don't worry about nothing
because God's got everything.

~Nancy Winningham~

You have to get to some ifs before
you can acquire certainties.

~Nancy Winningham~

The enemy tries but God does.
~Nancy Winningham~

My vision establishes my mission.
~Nancy Winningham~

If it is not showing, I know
where one may not be going.

~Nancy Winningham~

If you can't take the time to give back,
you need to get back.

~Nancy Winningham~

You may have taken a U-Turn,
it is now your turn.
~Nancy Winningham~

No mess in the process.
~Nancy Winningham~

Prayer over powers poison.
~Nancy Winningham~

Expect some testing while
waiting on a blessing.
~Nancy Winningham~

The reactions to distractions
have consequences.
~Nancy Winningham~

Peace brings on a sacred moment.
~Nancy Winningham~

Keeping the faith is a
reflection of your future.

~Nancy Winningham ~

Joy equals peace and peace
brings on understanding.

~Nancy Winningham~

God will turn your obstacles
into opportunities.
~Nancy Winningham~

Thoughts are inner feelings
that have implication.
~Nancy Winningham~

A trial is not meant to cause
pain but it does serve as an
umbrella during the rain.

~Nancy Winningham~

A manipulator can sometimes show
to be an instigator but at the end
of the day he is my motivator.

~Nancy Winningham~

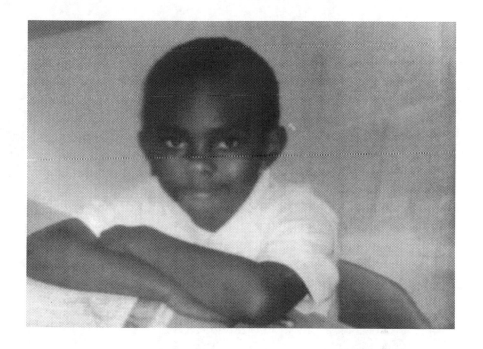

If your child struggles with the
way he learns, I suggest you teach
him the way he can learn.

~Nancy Winningham~

Thank God through every circumstance.
~Nancy Winningham~

I can look back but I don't
have to go back!
~Nancy Winningham~

To welcome your soul mate one would
have to unwelcome old baggage.

~Nancy Winningham~

Anytime you are not blindsided
by the word you will not be
blindsided by the world.

~Nancy Winningham~

Thanking God daily shows
continuous faith in him.

~Nancy Winningham~

God is a demonstrator as
well as an eliminator.

~Nancy Winningham~

One's daily life is a reminder
of God's goodness.
~Nancy Winningham~

Real love is destined to happen.
~Nancy Winningham~

Prayer plus faith equals assurance.
~Nancy Winningham~

Love is perpetual.
~Nancy Winningham~

Love comes from within.
~Nancy Winningham~

I am ready for the enemy but the enemy is not ready for me.

~Nancy Winningham~

Satisfaction brings comfort.

~Nancy Winningham~

Happiness is like a candle burning
in an endless candle flame.

~Nancy Winningham~

God reminds me of a cell phone
provider, He has an unlimited plan.

~Nancy Winningham~

Life experiences
will result in alterations.
~Nancy Winningham~

Mistakes are expected
but change is much needed.
~Nancy Winningham~

God reminds me of a
mathematical equation, He has
a solution to every problem.

~Nancy Winningham~

The choices you make are a
reflection of your future.

~Nancy Winningham~

Ceaseless love is the best love.
~Nancy Winningham~

A man who loves God will
definitely love you.
~Nancy Winningham~

Facing up to your trials will
make you stronger.
~Nancy Winningham~

Peace within shows ease.
~Nancy Winningham~

God reminds me of Campbell soup,
He is mmm mmm good.

~Nancy Winningham~

God reminds me of a delete key, He
will remove those who don't belong.

~Nancy Winningham~

The enjoyment of giving makes
my life worth living.
~Nancy Winningham~

God preserves what you deserve.
~Nancy Winningham~

God reminds me of a see saw,
when I am down He will pull me up.

~Nancy Winningham~

God reminds me of a computer,
He has an abundance of memory space.

~Nancy Winningham~

Your decision determines your vision.
~Nancy Winningham~

Contentment unlocks the
door to good health.
~Nancy Winningham~

Live life and don't let it live you.
~Nancy Winningham~

The act of caring for others shows
God lives inside of you.
~Nancy Winningham~

When a man loves his wife as Christ loves the church, his home will always be filled with love.

~Nancy Winningham~

I am glad that God is the CEO of the company that I work for.

~Nancy Winningham~

I'm not tripping but I am praying.
~Nancy Winningham~

Forgiveness is an internal relief.
~Nancy Winningham~

A lack of knowledge
equals a lack of understanding.

~Nancy Winningham~

Goals are optional but achieving
them is mandatory.

~Nancy Winningham~

Success is what you make it.
~Nancy Winningham~

Excellence is obtainable but
disobedience is not an option.
~Nancy Winningham~

Today is a different day and it is always better than the last.
~Nancy Winningham~

There is work in a blessing.
~Nancy Winningham~

I love a challenge, it is when I
don't receive one is what concerns me.
~Nancy Winningham~

Choices are individualized.
~Nancy Winningham~

One's daily life is a
reminder of God's goodness.

~Nancy Winningham~

I don't speak the impossible
but I speak the possible.

~Nancy Winningham~

Never present promises
because your options are limited.
~Nancy Winningham~

With true love there are sacrifices.
~Nancy Winningham~

Collaboration equals dedication.
~Nancy Winningham~

While the enemy is playing,
I am praying.
~Nancy Winningham~

Behind every struggle is a blessing.
~Nancy Winningham~

While the enemy is preying,
I am praying.
~Nancy Winningham~

I can maintain self-control
without taking control.
~Nancy Winningham~

With every challenge there is a reward.
~Nancy Winningham~

Let your obstacles be your roadmap toward your endeavors.

~Nancy Winningham~

God does not need to trust us, we need to trust God.

~Nancy Winningham~

Love is immeasurable.
~Nancy Winningham~

God reminds me of the sun,
He brightens up my day.
~Nancy Winningham~

God reminds me of a Duracell battery,
He keeps going and going and going.

~Nancy Winningham~

God reminds me of the time, He doesn't
wait on us instead we wait on him.

~Nancy Winningham~

God reminds me of an editor,
He will edit your life.
~Nancy Winningham~

God reminds me of a 24 hour answering
service, He always answers every call.
~Nancy Winningham~

A vision expands into a mission.
~Nancy Winningham~

Serenity brings peace.
~Nancy Winningham~

God will give you more
than you had before.

~Nancy Winningham~

Never attempt to make sense
out of foolishness.

~Nancy Winningham~

God had a strategy
and now I have a story.
~Nancy Winningham~

My divorce was final a long time ago
and the ground was negative people.
~Nancy Winningham~

God provided me with the vision to move forward toward the mission.
~Nancy Winningham~

God has a strategy for my tragedy.
~Nancy Winningham~

A loving heart shows a loving spirit.
~Nancy Winningham~

When you delay you may
forget what you say.
~Nancy Winningham~

Preparation establishes restoration.
~Nancy Winningham~

To be sacrificial is not beneficial.
~Nancy Winningham~

God never practices exclusion,
He focuses on inclusion.
~Nancy Winningham~

God makes a way every day.
~Nancy Winningham~

Don't let someone else's foolishness disturb your happiness.
~Nancy Winningham~

Favor aint fair but it's there.
~Nancy Winningham~

Be thankful, trustful, and never doubtful to God's word.

~Nancy Winningham~

A person who puts energy into foolishness shows to have no sense.

~Nancy Winningham~

Drama is for TV and I am
not part of the sitcom.
~Nancy Winningham~

God is who He says He is.
~Nancy Winningham~

God I know the things that's happening
is by your grace; I thank you for
directing me while I run this race.
~Nancy Winningham~

Man rejects while God protects.
~Nancy Winningham~

Think it, organize it, and apply it.
~Nancy Winningham~

I thank God for this **GIFT.**

God Is Full Time
~Nancy Winningham~

God is love with no epidemics;
He is one we should all mimic.

~Nancy Winningham~

People who are miserable throughout a
given day will attempt to take you
with them if you entertain every
word they have to say.

~Nancy Winningham~

God protects his saints and when you don't know what direction to go just remember his GPS will let you know that **God Protects** his **Saints**.

~Nancy Winningham~

Don't get frustrated when trials come your way, instead embrace them all and know tomorrow is a different day.

~Nancy Winningham~

Never focus on negative words
that people say about you, instead
continue to do what God says do.

~Nancy Winningham~

Your past confirms you, your present
calms you, your future formulates you.

~Nancy Winningham~

God protects and He never neglects.
~Nancy Winningham~

Let your light shine no matter how
vague you think it may be, always
believe that God has given it
to you so others may see.

~Nancy Winningham~

It is known that one's life could be hard,
it is a written fact that everything
should be left up to God.

~Nancy Winningham~

When I think of the challenges
that God allows me to face, I thank
him for giving me the strength
to begin and finish the race.

~Nancy Winningham~

There is no need to stress
during the mess instead praise
God throughout the process.

~Nancy Winningham~

Don't stick around when one is
trying to pull you down.

~Nancy Winningham~

Because you are going through
means God is working for you.

~Nancy Winningham~

While the enemy is messing God
is blessing in the right direction.

~Nancy Winningham~

I thank God for every test because
I know that God knows best.

~Nancy Winningham~

Without a trial my life
would definitely be wild.

~Nancy Winningham~

Without a test my life would be a mess.
~Nancy Winningham~

The enemy can have an attitude,
the enemy can be rude, but one thing
for sure the enemy will never
disturb my pleasant mood.

~Nancy Winningham~

Everybody who pats your back
are not always where you're at.
~Nancy Winningham~

I told the enemy to get back due to
a holdup and now I have an
outstanding come up.
~Nancy Winningham~

When I look in the mirror there are two words that describe me and they are grace and mercy.

~Nancy Winningham~

When I am informed it is time for me to transform.

~Nancy Winningham~

Man can delete me but my
God always completes me.

~Nancy Winningham~

I had a temporary breakdown, which
allowed me to have a brief shut down
but God's grace turned it around.

~Nancy Winningham~

With God everyone's included
and nobody is excluded.

~Nancy Winningham~

I am so thankful that God is the
CEO of the company I work for;
He has an open door policy.

~Nancy Winningham~

My glory tells my story.
~Nancy Winningham~

God is and He does.
~Nancy Winningham~

God plans my day and
renovates my past.
~Nancy Winningham~

Prayer changes my position.
~Nancy Winningham~

Use one's strength to
overpower the weakness.
~Nancy Winningham~

Through all of my mess God always
provides me with a message.
~Nancy Winningham~

Parents
Raising
All
Youth
~Nancy Winningham~

When the enemy tries to be
deceptive God intercepts.

~Nancy Winningham~

Chasing the storm makes you stronger.
~Nancy Winningham~

I have a story so I have no choice
but to give God the glory.
~Nancy Winningham~